BLACK DOG DRINKING FROM AN OUTDOOR POOL

Black Dog Drinking from an Outdoor Pool
Copyright © 2019 by Zach Ozma

Cover photograph by Eva Gibeau. Used by permission.
Author photograph by Ellis Martin.
Cover design by Seth Pennington.

All rights reserved. No part of this book may be reproduced or republished without written consent from the publisher, except by reviewers who may quote brief excerpts in connection with a review in a newspaper, magazine, or electronic publication; nor may any part of this book be reproduced, stored in a retrieval system, or transmitted in any form, or by any means be recorded without written consent of the publisher.

Sibling Rivalry Press, LLC
PO Box 26147
Little Rock, AR 72221

info@siblingrivalrypress.com

www.siblingrivalrypress.com

ISBN: 978-1-943977-56-7

Library of Congress Control No: 2018960675

By special invitation, this title is housed in the Rare Book and Special Collections Vault of the Library of Congress.

First Sibling Rivalry Press Edition, March 2019

BLACK DOG DRINKING FROM AN OUTDOOR POOL

ZACH OZMA

SIBLING RIVALRY PRESS
DISTURB / ENRAPTURE
LITTLE ROCK / ARKANSAS

CONTENTS

13	Source Material
14	Daddy Tell Me the One about the Wild Dogs
16	Dog's Wet Mouth
17	See Spot
27	Garbage Man
28	Garbage Men
29	A New World Where All Things Are Possible
33	1
34	Ways This Transformation May Have Happened
42	Matters of the House as Not Yet Addressed
48	In Which the Dog Moves to the Big City Part One
51	Contingencies
52	In Which the Dog Moves to the Big City Part Two
57	Wikipedia Knew my Dad Was Dead Before I Knew My Dad Was Dead
58	Calla Lily
68	My Dad's Black Cat Drops Dead After Five Years of Drinking from the Pool
73	I'm Triggered by Your Triggers
78	Dog Rounds Block on Bicycle Sixteen Times and Doesn't Sniff a Soul
81	Happy Dogyear
84	Mud and Butter
88	There's No Dog in this Poem but Me
94	Every Famous Dog You Know Is Already Dead
95	The Dogfather
96	Dog Coffee
98	Black Dog Goes Home
103	Epilogue

*For Shep, my father's father
and Duke, my father's shepherd*

and for my mother who told me to tell it any way I wanted

what do you want to be, a garbage man?
    words from father's father to father, 1968

a new world where all things are possible
    words from father to mother, 1988

SOURCE MATERIAL

if a dog is in no way like his father, there's a dead cat on the line

DADDY TELL ME THE ONE ABOUT THE WILD DOGS

good boy leaves house
to rove town with pack of wild dogs
because it is easy

eats trash sleeps in rolling fields of the west
drives blue pickup truck to county dump
oooo-ooooh garbage

night comes good boy howls with others
while over mountain bottleneck
slides across perfectly tuned river

good boy misses low pile carpet
good boy misses fire
good boy is not good boy anymore

good boy is baaaaaad dog
wild dogs want to come over later
piss in pool, muck up carpet, empty fridge

good boy wears suit of linen and mud-caked fur
wrecks family car
wants bath but can't say so

begs hamburger from bartender at one-eyed mike's
shocks at proximity before meal is served
learns how many ways a boy can leave a valley

look: you are dog and i am mud
every pooch tells this story the same

DOG'S WET MOUTH

the post office was adhesive
and dog licked stamps

                    the international father fan club
                    kept sending things to eat

SEE SPOT

father said the sunspots were cancerous

wife called and said it was his heart

we lied and said the dog doesn't bite

the paper said father was a genius. verbatim

the social worker said it was ok for them to keep the dog

he asked if i remembered what father's hands and feet looked like

he said a pisces always killed himself in a past life

father told his father he didn't know how to act

father's father told him to fake it till you make it

dog didn't know how to not act like dog

dog comes out of the neighbor's kitchen

with a round raw burger patty in dog's lithe mouth

father never wore sunscreen on long island

he said the spots were cancerous

broke his own rib from exertion

blackberry stigmata on those brilliantly blessed palms

father wanted mother

father wanted dog

he wanted the endless want of children and fathers and dogs

the top three creatures least likely to know when enough is enough

beef fat on all three of their semitic lips

we lied and said father doesn't bite

we faked it

                                                we secreted things in cupboards

                                                       took turns writing notes

father's father had three strokes and lives

until he cannot choose between dialysis and jacket potatoes

father lives until somebody tells

we faked it

we majored in ethnomusicology, in fine arts

dog didn't go to school, just licked and licked
      until those skin spots

   glowed with their own california sunlight

mother said father wanted to be a good father

but even good dogs can't stop wanting

mother said he loved his garden

mother said he loved his dog

dog doesn't know what to love yet

dog tries to love the plums

the low pile carpet

the blackberries cooking on summer driveway like eggs

the social worker told them they were allowed to keep the dog

GARBAGE MAN

father accuses mother of an affair with the garbage man

but it's dog that licks the slime from between

the trash collector's wicked fingers

GARBAGE MEN

on that precipice of transfer station
eau de hot garbage, behind ears, inner wrists
century plant at entrance spinning a careening spin
to milky blue of heavens otherwise

i became a garbage man, a trash santa,

tiny, in my miniature leather work shoes

paws of my body reaching skyward in
heavenly emulation of the vaporous odors
light filtering thru corrugated roof
despicable green density of the mountain

black plastic so sticky drool runs down to my ankles

my useless boy nose, unable to quite reach the source

A NEW WORLD WHERE ALL THINGS ARE POSSIBLE
or
MY FATHER TAUGHT ME THAT I SHOULD PRUNE THE PLUM TREE BUT NOT HOW

Father says, "You are not enough mother for me! How will you bandage all my cracked and laborious fingers? How will you put up all the plums I have so carefully coaxed from the tree and made plump and sugary with my diligent pruning? How will you hear my beautiful songs with your ears all full of Cole Porter? How will you tell me I am good while you are busy telling dog he *is good? I am going away for a while and when I return it will be to a new world where all things are possible."*

Mother waterfalls her beautiful hair over one shoulder and narrows her grey and close-together eyes, says nothing. She turns the ring in slow circles around her dish-softened finger and looks father in the eye. The rivulets that form between her brows are licked smooth by pup tongue.

Father goes to the airport and the redwood-beamed house at last lays still. All day long in the velvet and sweltering living room, mother gives birth to more mothers. One by one, her feet jammed in hot black shoes. Little plum slicks soak the floor. Mother's linen dress drenched in fructose and placenta.

At first, dog sniffs at the baby mothers. Dog chances licks at their gooey-slicked beautiful hair, their close-together eyes soaked shut, the round and womanly proportions of their sumptuous baby fat bodies. After a few tastes, dog with suspicious backward glance, pads down to asphalt front yard. Turns lazy, looks up to plum trees lining driveway, fresh green twigs already growing past their bounds.

Inside, mother pants in the heat. Baby mothers line the velvet upholstery. Baby mothers all in the glass front built-ins; these ones are instructed to touch nothing but their own slick spines. A single very small and plump baby mother turns at 78 revolutions per minute on the record player which father has left on to keep mother company. Mother pants in the heat. Plaits her hair. One by one more baby mothers are born, plump and round and the color of stone fruits.

Dog and cat curl together in the driveway. Dog thought cat had gotten blue and left but cat is back again. House full of baby mothers, no room for pups or pussies. Cat lies languid but dog is rigid with concern for the plum trees. Fruits burst forth in clusters. Dog knows plums will not sweeten this way. Father's pruning shears rusty gleam from porch and dog looks at dog's own clumsy paws. Where to cut? What to take?

Cat dreams that mother has a plum for a belly. Cat is a fool, and dog pads inside to coolness of kitchen. Upon closer inspection the white tile runs with coral veins. Each night, the sink polished to a plum glow. Dog presses face to floor but heat of the plum worry presses on dog. Redwood-beamed ceiling seems to swell with juice, as if the lacquer a thin skin. Mother gives birth to baby mothers, one by one. With half-closed eyes, a baby mother toddles and rolls over to dog, presses two sticky fingers into the wet pink space visible between dog's drooping jowls. She tastes of sweet hot rot and a sugary bee sting. Dog bristles, shakes it off, pads outside. Baby mothers bob in chlorinated and body temperature water of the pool. Sun glints off water making alien lines on their faces. Cat has ditched the scene. Baby mothers doze on hood of car. Maroon finish shines in heavy, placid sunlight. Mother gathers stone fruits in sideyard. She shines car and baby mothers with waxy skins, plump with juice. They will glisten for father with her spite.

Dog sleeps fitfully in shade of plum tree. Inside, walls have swollen with juice. Father will return to a house full and fat and wet and plum trees will not have been pruned and there will be too many plums, too many baby mothers, and dog will have to bandage father's fingers. The baby mother's ears are too slick with fruity flesh to hear father's mournful songs. How do baby mothers manage to be so round and so adultlike at once? Mother cradles each succulent homunculus to her breast.

On hardwood credenza, father's photos are all coral toned. Mother puts on a record, gives birth to a few more baby mothers, licks sweet pulp from their faces. Did she have father? Did she have dog? She has built a choir of baby mothers and they will make beautiful music and go on a world tour in their shiny plum car and no one will put up fruits of the field and no one will bandage father's fingers and dog (if there had ever been a dog) will roam the valley with a pack of feral pups and never have to learn to prune even one plum tree and no one, no one will be a good boy. That is, when the baby mothers finally cough up phlegmy pulpy plum wine fermenting in their throats.

Mother combs her long beautiful black hair, dreams of the new world where all things are possible.

The baby mothers begin to congeal.

Dog wakes with a start as plum after plum tumbles from tree and batters dog's slick black body. A single baby mother lifts her bruised head from fruit pile and coughs a phlegmy pit into her pink hand. Dog gets one sniff and turns, whining, back to house. Dog squeezes dog's dog body in between wet, crushing sugared walls. Redwood beams give a little with even slightest pressure. A darkness almost unnavigable. In velvet living room, mother combs her beautiful wet hair. Dog lets out low whine but mother does not turn head. Baby mothers are secreting each loose strand of mother's hair, covering their faces until they look like dogs. Dog buries dog's face in wet wall, comes out looking like a juicy baby.

Miles down hot and devilish highway, an airplane is landing. Father grips armrest with his cracked and calloused fingers. Whispers in time with rumbling jets, "A new world, a new world, a new world."

1

please i am sorry:

    this is my first time being dog

i try to comb the mud out of my fur
                              i mean
dog combs mud from dog's bristled fur
                              i mean

    our haunches leave imprints on the low pile white carpet

                              i mean
i don't know the manners and customs yet

coiled in that secret spot where it gives way to tile
                              i mean

        the panting breath of me
        me slipping out my wrists and back

i didn't not making anything   i mean
sour cream and bananas

or mud i guess

    either way it leaves soft impressions in my fur

WAYS THIS TRANSFORMATION MAY HAVE HAPPENED

mother waited so long until the coffee got cold
cannot become a dog at all

boy fills bathtub with espresso sinks meager winter-skinned boy body into frothy thick-dark surface comes out a wagging-dripping pup

mother slips sour plum slices into pancakes, pastas
but boy is onto her
hugs pancakes to his chest, pasta around his genitals
climbs into compost bin and doesn't come back

father drives panting mother to the hospital
but winds up outside the pound

dog arrives upside down, three days early
covered in placenta

there was never any such thing as a daughter

in the basement, father blew puppies out of smoke

the valley burned all summer
the pregnant ladies gave birth to soot

MATTERS OF THE HOUSE AS NOT YET ADDRESSED

how many holes in this house
how many holes in a dog

dog name burned into the deck
do you know the way way way way

dog with keys to the house
dog with facial moisturizer from the big mall in San Jose

loma prieta
melanoma prieta

little smear of dog blood
on white tile

woody
-goody

cotton
alliums cooked in oil

still in fireplace night time
cricket tick through window

glimpse other side of chin
peeping skillet bottom or

good door to be closed
good boy still on carpet

slippery dog offal
slippery plum rub

depends on the house

depends on the dog

IN WHICH THE DOG MOVES TO THE BIG CITY
PART ONE

Wild nights are my glory.
  Madeleine L'Engle, *A Wrinkle in Time*

So I left, the stars were shining
  like the lights around a swimming pool
    Frank O'Hara, "Ode to Michael Goldberg
    ('s Birth and Other Births)"

the wild dogs loot stores on wild nights
licking up the storm because they have no father

because the wild dogs said "i will not become the mother"
and so their tongues grew flat and long and
pink (flocked ribbons) and their voices grew loud and
strange and they abdicated the linen pants and salade niçoise
for wetter frothier clothes of the northern hills

wild dogs not mother at all but freeway
not father at all but chicken bones stacked in the night

black dog cannot or won't not understand that dog
was child and then boy and then not mother but dog
black dog cannot or won't not know that lapping at thick
and heavy mugs is no balm at all for the father fingers
unfurling from dog's own dog paws

the wild dogs will make it in this gate eventually
and then this whole house will fall in the mud

dogs don't eat plums because
a plum pit will cling to tongue
until they remember how to speak
like their mother

this is the only way back but
back no way at all
mother must take off her black shoes
to cross low pile carpet

father places an international phone call
but wild dogs are tying up the line

CONTINGENCIES

if dog comes back here
what kind of reception will he receive

as dog is known to be a ne'er-do-well
and an outlaw

and stands in opposition to all our
good and true family values

dog, who has outstanding medical debts, dog
who may appear to be a man in a tailored suit

but who can't even play one swing chord
on his inherited guitar

IN WHICH THE DOG MOVES TO THE BIG CITY
PART TWO

> *When I said I wanted to be your dog*
> *I wasn't coming on to you*
> *I just wanted to lick your face*
>   Jens Lekman

mother smooths black dog's ears feeds dog black plum
chlorinated juice sterilizes dog's luscious garbage insides
dog's dog organs shed their silky mucilaginous coating
at last it is revealed to everyone that dog's dog organs are baby-sized

little pit-sized baby heart and little pit-sized baby liver
little pit-sized baby kidneys knocking around
in dog's big ribcage, dog's water-filled gut

dog shaves dog's face in father's mirror
comes out a moneyed and well-mannered son

son and mother touch elbows on the couch
mother sings the one about the wild dogs
son's pit-sized baby belly growls

dog quits his job and grows a little beard
sleeps with hand on lover's chest
carries keys on rightmost belt loop
rolls over for anyone who asks

WIKIPEDIA KNEW MY DAD WAS DEAD BEFORE I KNEW MY DAD WAS DEAD

category: suicides by method

---

this article includes a list of references, but its sources remain unclear

the suicide rates by domestic gas fell from 1960 to 1980.[96]

if you are a person who often travels out of town	●	you should not have a dog
you should know where all the main shut offs are in your house	○ ○ ○	for water for electric for gas

this list may not reflect recent changes (learn more)

remember, the fan club is your next of kin

CALLA LILY

when i was small enough for california to still have water

when i was small enough to still be small

instead i grow dog-sized

the san lorenzo curls to the side

drive highway length

pull up to gate

bar door with tourmaline

for years slice of graham hill road: s-curves

three diamond signs: yellow. down pull of forest: more than

gravity. back seat of volvo peeping mirror for just lips and that's all

dream is over when you get dry

dog of my body curls gingerly to the side, lacquers every inch

i swim in the murky ocean and after, a single breast

bristle my hairs and learn big dog teeth better now

father is there at the hinged post

rests his chin on the back of my neck

wake jerky and coniferous

to someone else's chin

we play old, house, dig garden to mud

look for brass tools to open gate

that's the game

it's difficult here to tell what but if predicted

mother warned me about the pacific undertow,
and i pictured him:

huge, slick-mud warted, under-toad grabs ankle
with webbed paw

mother warns me about a dream she had when young

follows good catholic boy with sheen of his tongue to hall closet

he shows his penis: slow handful of worms many twisting

that's the joke

the name of this place: pronounced with resignation

calla lilies cluster along worried drainline

it's difficult here to tell when but if practiced

nose at worm pile with dog snout

paw at wet and panting earth

predictions made of shape of outline of body:

discovered later to be ok

pant in the heat

roll over

shade the skin of my grease

MY DAD'S BLACK CAT DROPS DEAD AFTER FIVE YEARS OF DRINKING FROM THE POOL

on the videotape
two boys submerged
long-haired plastic-pearled
in giraffed pool light

changing together in blue tile bathroom
after swimming
two puff of hair
inexplicable
dog knew the secret between my legs

dog walks five miles on highway to my front door
fireworks make afraid
but not so much as gasoline start to backyard burnpile

father's dog died when i was born
house too small for many pups
dog curled up in mud
became a redwood

i curled up in low pile carpet
became a boy

cat licks butter from kitchen counter
cat licks cat from limp tail
cast iron skillet for eggs and that's all

is it better to be an egg or a skillet
is it better to be a boy or a redwood
is it better to be a cat or a pool
is it better to be a father or a dog

bay laurel drop leaf to pool surface then sink
he gives me quarters to fish them out again
each drenched leaf pressed to tankini skin
grows quiet fur patch

until i learn to bristle at the touch

I'M TRIGGERED BY YOUR TRIGGERS

wisteria hangs low
from aching body of house
i am bandaging father's calloused fingers

pisces water
pisces steel

jasmine bloom stickied finger
honeysuckle
key lime balm

when sun is clouded but sky free of trail
father will wander field of yard for hours
barefoot
i will prone on basement floor until night
counting each loop of low pile white carpet that touches skin

night falls so lie tucked up next to sweaty ceiling
each pore adjusted to emergency

pisces makes desperate assumption
it's 2015 in california and everyone i know has PTSD
even the dogs

high pile of the bathmat in high arch of
bare foot

mother's foot
father's earlobe

as far as anyone can tell it has always been this way

before dinner didn't know the words after did
strings of angel hair pasta each one made by hand
spun belly full of cursive

i learn it better
neosporin
cloth bandaid
the good stuff
i'm sorry
a balm
i'm sorry

each finger cracked

the work in father's hands

every pisces has a wet mouth
every instinct is a balm
every sorry is a sorrrry

tell me what hurts
walk the pasture
a musty black dog
a dog in my balm
yellowjacket in the ointment
black cherry soda on the sting

pisces cries mother into phone screen
i smooth ache out of doorway with hands
i baking soda each grout

slow

when house is empty of foot

i chlorinate myself blue for california
trace it in carpet
put it away

i learn to have mother's hands
finally
no daughter but a mother
no son but a mother

i clay my face into a useful shaped vessel
i learn it better

bandage my fingers too big to tell apart

DOG ROUNDS BLOCK ON BICYCLE SIXTEEN TIMES AND DOESN'T SNIFF A SOUL

those crackling voices turning
in circles once again as if a loma prieta
didn't topple father's records on top
of mother's 1947 gibson guitar

as if no collision had happened at all
everyone encased in puppy fat or
bubble wrapped like tchotchkes taken from
shelves in advance of a writhing storm

if we should pause here, aware, that's all
what is called *a learning moment*
everyone in california
calls their father an earthquake

if i have to choose, i always pick summer
through that unbreathable heat
tempered only by submersion
in a glistening sting of pool

or otherwise the jasmine chokes
fleas brushed from legs
pooling in the nooks and crannies
a swelter

pull the bad specks from dog's pale belly
one by one they scatter and pop
their vinyl exoskeletons turning
grooves etched too small to read

HAPPY DOGYEAR

california holiday

fathers grilling hamburgers
on the hoods of cars
foot tap in ⅔ time to
wailing wall of
carbon monoxide detector

dog has seven newyears
all at once
like being pelted
with hail
or rice

at midnight dog will be able
to speak in a man's voice
for a moment for
just long enough
for auld lang syne

until the beef father lips
clamp over dog's own
just long enough
for the bovine fat
to leave them wet

choking down the tuberose
should old dog be forgot
and never brought to mind
should old dog be forgot
and never brought to mind

MUD AND BUTTER

the part of me that is a dog knows that part of you is a pat of butter
i mean dog combs out mud from dog's bristled fur
the part of me that is a dog burnt my finger on the match
i mean dog is an outlaw and ne'er-do-well

i mean dog combs out mud from dog's bristled fur
i mean i hug the pat of butter to my chest
i mean dog is an outlaw and ne'er-do-well
i mean i turn myself inside out to be good

i mean i hug the pat of butter to my chest
the part of me that is a dog has buttercups on his breastbone
i mean i turn myself inside out to be good
the part of me that is a dog sweats through my sweater

the part of me that is a dog has buttercups on his breastbone
the part of me that is a dog burnt my finger on the match
the part of me that is a dog sweats through my sweater
the part of me that is a dog knows that part of you is a pat of butter

THERE'S NO DOG IN THIS POEM BUT ME

wife will hate you for shoveling
chicken shit in your stage shoes
and stage pants
and no shirt
and no socks

but this will be the father that is likable at least
with pruning shears
plum juice dripping on driveway
caterwaul from sideyard
blue egg

he crouches in walkways and stacks rocks
down up the size of babies
down to the size of child's clench fist
you call them earthquake detectors but
we will know

blackberry climbs fence wall
poison oak climbs fence hill
honeysuckle climbs fence tree
father climbs stairs with dirty feet
father climbs no oak for summer at all

you are safe bet in out of doors
fig tree leaks irritant sap
outside there is no singing
outside just bird tree cat hill
none at all

fire leaps to peer over hilltops
pill bugs roll like pin heads or
toxic berries secreted between toes
the prunings all have wet ends
the summers all have chlorine and canna pods

EVERY FAMOUS DOG YOU KNOW IS ALREADY DEAD

dog pisses in every room of the house
i sleep with my finger tip between his teeth
comforted only by a vague threat of injury

      oh laika oh otis oh beethoven oh sandy oh toto
      a tragic little wet spot on the carpet for each one

here is the sure thing about being a dog
or being a father: we will get on without you

      i wanted to be the first animal to orbit this house

that smell dog got in his last days—
already overripe, paws in glacial waters,
clumps of hairs excusing themselves one
by one, encased in cream rinse
dried to an oily glaze

      i wanted to do something nice: dog had
      so little time left to live

the father fingers already pressing up against
the inside of dog's dog skin

THE DOGFATHER

this is the story:

all dogs forgot to grow up but
in the future they will remember
walk on hind legs through
post offices and supermarkets

hold pens in cornchip-smelling paws
write notes to their wives
disappoint their children

smash windows of hot cars
die of asphyxiation on purpose

DOG COFFEE

before long it became a question of milk or not milk
coffee that's inevitable but choice, that's important
in the morning the pool will be full of blue milk
like a Hockney but with dogs instead of men

dogs on floaties dogs at the cold brew bar
dogs on the train dogs at their dog jobs
dogs posting on dogslist for other dogs

dog does best not to learn to operate espresso machine
even grown dog will pour-over, french press
things that can be done with these sleek and devilish paws

in the end there will be no workaround—the pool water
as wet and brown as dog's dumb eyes
california sunrise steam to break even
first dog gets dog spots and then dog was black dog all along

shiny black dog coat washed with anti-odor dog shampoo
shiny black pitcher of wet foggy cream
two-tone dog claws tap on stoneware mug
doggy milk teeth sharp down to nothing

BLACK DOG GOES HOME

this is the story:

everyone who has a father gets a dog instead
but it still goes sour

everyone unadoptable

good boy

unadoptable pup sink tongue to black cherry soda
lap at tile floor

good *boy*–

i'm a dog i'm a dog i'm a dog i'm

steel strings make crisscross with grout
a father sings in low and stolen tones
this is all fathers are allowed to do now

dog is good replacement father mostly by looking at you
with wet eyes and saying nothing

dog drives you to the prom and drops you off around the corner

dog is like father in that they are a known quantity until they are not

dog gets too hungry and takes a bite right out of you, son

good boy

dark and sweltering living room
maroon velveteen upholstery
favorite and most dramatic record
think i'll eat some tinsel, some trash

good boy

i'm a dog i'm a dog i'm a dog i'm a dog

dog is lousy breadwinner
dog is lousy man
dog gets mention in local paper, pisses inside
dog doesn't know when we're going home until it's too late

father slimes face in compost pile
father licks himself clean
father curls up by fire
father crawls under house to die

EPILOGUE

In the new world where all things are possible, there are no fathers at all. Instead of father's day, we have dog's day. Instead of father time we have dog time. Instead of the father, the son, and the holy ghost, we have three dogs in a sleek oroborus of sniffing.

At first, this was a difficult adjustment. We didn't know if dog would be able to drive the cars the way fathers had. But then the volvo company made some special super safe family innovations on their special super safe family cars, so the dogs (even the small dogs) could reach the pedals and grasp the steering wheels (even though most of the dogs who replaced our fathers were large; sleek muscular black furry things).

Dog turns around six times in bed, rests heavy head on mother's thigh like a cut of meat at the butcher. Eventually mother got used to that too.

Once there were dogfathers, we didn't have to be pups anymore. We got to shave the hair from our faces, walk upright, eyes in the sun. That took some adjusting too, learning to throw our shoulders back and walk with that invisible string from the crowns of our heads again. Stop sniffing each other in alleyways. You feel like a person, and then you catch the wrong glimpse in a store window or in someone's reflective sun lenses. And then you have to find some other poor stray who's having a hard time switching back to being a son, rub up against each other awhile, pant in the glorious horrible heat of each other's skin and hair and teeth. And when you had slunk back to your man clothes and your man shoes and said your furtive goodbyes, you would not call him. We called that ghosting. Sometimes, in the half-light of his bedroom, his beard on the back of your neck would feel like father. We called that ghosting too.

You couldn't find plums anymore. Not even in the big specialty store by the train tracks where they have sixteen kinds of feta cheese in little plastic wrappers. We talked about the plums in hushed voices, the way someone who doesn't drink anymore might glow over the imagining of it, a paper cup of shit coffee in her hand instead of alcohol.

The fathers sang on the radio, low. This was a good use of father's special skills. Dog bristled with the radio on, turned against the grumbling wall of sounds. We learned to turn the radio off when dog came in the room, and this made us feel at home too. Nothing feels so much like father as having something to hide. Mother pretends not to like the radio sounds either, until we catch her in the bathtub with the little battery operated one, hugging it greedily, animal teeth showing through the revlon on her lips. Mother is trying to teach dog to play the piano, but he won't have it.

Dog keeps trying to die, and that reminds us of father too. We keep extra keys to the car secreted in our clothes for when he locks himself inside on summer days. He keeps embarrassing us, with his stupid paws, and wet pink hard-on, and how he makes small talk with our friends. Dog keeps pissing on everything, but he's sorry, we're sorry, we're all so very very sorry. We can't really blame him for this: he didn't ask to be a dog. That is something we can understand. He makes terrible coffee. He talks about himself a lot less than father did.

There's sweetness too: in the wet nudge of his dog nose to wake us. The way, when we drive home, he pulls the car into the driveway, lets us put the front seats down and stay for a while, tells us how beautiful *we are in the green underwater light of the dash. We ask if dog remembers plums; he says nothing. Dog always says nothing.*

In the yard, the pool gleams in the restless sunlight.

We skim the water for hair, great soft wet sticky clumps of the stuff. In the cool darkness of the evenings—when at last we are alone, no mother at all, no father at all, not even a dog to lap our salty skin—we press the chlorinated fur to our faces, turn around six times in bed, sleep.

ACKNOWLEDGMENTS

The book that you are holding would not exist without the tireless editing assistance of my partner Julian Shendelman and the trust and support of Bryan Borland and Seth Pennington of Sibling Rivalry Press. Thank you for shepherding (haha) my first book in the world.

Thank you to my poetry steadies: Britt Billmeyer-Finn, Cheena Marie Lo, and Tessa Micaela Landreau-Grasmuck. I owe a debt of gratitude especially to Zoe Tuck, who introduced me to all these other loved ones; who pushes me to make better, stranger work; who said "careful, if you keep coming to these poetry readings someone will eventually ask you to read, so you're going to have to start writing poetry."

The earliest mention of the black dog is in a note from a materialist poetry exercise in a class taught by Dario Robleto in the Shaklee Building at California College of the Arts in Oakland in 2014. Thank you to Dario and the other materialist poets who filled that classroom with your words and work– particularly Lukaza Branfman-Verissimo, Shushan Tesfuzigta, Tania Butterworth, Caroline Weaver, Maio Alvear, Mo Nuñez, Petter Dahlström Persson, and Indira Allegra.

Thank you to my mother, CJ MacDuffee, for teaching me to live a writer's life, both when it is fruitful and when it is messy and slow. Thank you to Georgie, black poodle of my childhood, and to Charlie and Ramona Pickle, the black dogs who rested their heads on me as I wrote this. Thank you to Noah Pellegrino, for editing my drafts and driving the getaway car. To Maxfield Orr, who saw it all from the very beginning. And to the countless others who have held me and this writing: thank you thank you thank you.

THE AUTHOR

Zach Ozma is a poet, potter, and social practice artist. He was born on dry land in Santa Cruz, CA and raised for a time in an adjacent mountain town. In 2015, Ozma received a BFA in Community Arts from California College of the Arts in Oakland. He is involved in a long-term embodied research practice in the Louis Graydon Sullivan Archive. Ozma has shown artwork at Nook Gallery, CTRL+SHFT Collective, and Artist Television Access. His writing has appeared in *Vetch Magazine*, *DATABLEED*, and *It's Night In San Francisco But It's Sunny in Oakland*. These days, he lives in Philadelphia with his partner Julian and their two rescue dogs, Charles and Frankie. Only one of the dogs likes to swim.

Black Dog Drinking from an Outdoor Pool is Ozma's first book.

THE COVER PHOTOGRAPHER

Eva Gibeau was born and raised in California. They received a BFA in Photography from California College of the Arts and they think about the light in California a lot.

THE PRESS

Sibling Rivalry Press is an independent press based in Little Rock, Arkansas. It is a sponsored project of Fractured Atlas, a nonprofit arts service organization. Contributions to support the operations of Sibling Rivalry Press are tax-deductible to the extent permitted by law, and your donations will directly assist in the publication of work that disturbs and enraptures. To contribute to the publication of more books like this one, please visit our website and click *donate*.

Sibling Rivalry Press gratefully acknowledges the following donors, without whom this book would not be possible:

Tony Taylor
Mollie Lacy
Karline Tierney
Maureen Seaton
Travis Lau
Michael Broder & Indolent Books
Robert Petersen
Jennifer Armour
Alana Smoot
Paul Romero
Julie R. Enszer
Clayton Blackstock
Tess Wilmans-Higgins & Jeff Higgins
Sarah Browning
Tina Bradley
Kai Coggin
Queer Arts Arkansas
Jim Cory
Craig Cotter
Hugh Tipping
Mark Ward

Russell Bunge
Joe Pan & Brooklyn Arts Press
Carl Lavigne
Karen Hayes
J. Andrew Goodman
Diane Greene
W. Stephen Breedlove
Ed Madden
Rob Jacques
Erik Schuckers
Sugar le Fae
John Bateman
Elizabeth Ahl
Risa Denenberg
Ron Mohring & Seven Kitchens Press
Guy Choate & Argenta Reading Series
Guy Traiber
Don Cellini
John Bateman
Gustavo Hernandez
Anonymous (12)

www.ingramcontent.com/pod-product-compliance
Lightning Source LLC
Chambersburg PA
CBHW030050100426
42734CB00038B/991